# THE 40-DAY ONSLAUGHT

*Before the Miraculous Divine Elevation*

Jessica AA Highsmith

*Before the Miraculous Divine Elevation*
Jessica AA Highsmith Copyright © 2024

**EMPOWER ME BOOKS, INC.**
*A Subsidiary of Empower Me Enterprises, Inc.*
https://www.empowermeenterprises.com

New International Version (NIV):
Scripture quotations taken from The Holy Bible, New International Version® NIV®. Copyright © 1973, 1978, 1984, 2011 by Biblica, Inc.® Used by permission. All rights reserved worldwide.

Amplified Bible (AMP):
Scripture quotations taken from the Amplified® Bible, Copyright © 2015 by The Lockman Foundation. Used by permission. All rights reserved.

The Message (MSG):
Scripture quotations taken from The Message. Copyright © 1993, 2002, 2018 by Eugene H. Peterson. Used by permission of NavPress. All rights reserved.

**ISBN: 978-1954418271**
**Printed in the United States of America**

First Edition: August 25, 2024

*I dedicate*

*this to the peculiar and*

*chosen generation like me*

*representing the Sonship of Christ!*

*Orphans Return to the Father,*

*He's Waiting on You ... Your*

*work is waiting on YOU!*

# CONTENTS

# CONTENTS

# FOREWORD

*ATV Ministries, Virgina USA*

The 40-Day Onslaught is a powerful testament to enduring and overcoming the tactics of the enemy. Spiritual warfare is real, but it cannot prevail against the Kingdom of God. There are two types of warfare we face: the kind we bring upon ourselves through disobedience, and the kind that arises simply because we are part of the Kingdom. To fully grasp this, we must understand the nature of warfare itself.

According to Webster, warfare is the act of engaging in or conducting conflict. Conflict is everywhere—some of it we initiate, and some we face due to who we are and who we represent. As Kingdom citizens, we will encounter spiritual warfare, but it cannot destroy us. Scripture assures us that while weapons may form, they will not prosper (Isaiah 54:17). We are surrounded by a divine shield of protection that deflects the enemy's attacks, and this shield is what Jessica Highsmith calls "Apostolic Resilience."

Jessica's journey is a living testament to the power of Apostolic Resilience. In this book, she provides not only her testimony but also a manual for defeating the enemy. Many claim to face spiritual warfare, but few truly know how to recover after being attacked. They engage in battle without armor, unprepared and unequipped, leading to defeat.

Yet, God's Word declares that we are victorious and more than conquerors (Romans 8:37). If we are victorious, defeat has no place in our story because God never lies. To walk in this victory, we must recognize the apostolic authority we've been given. This authority allows us to command and demand according to God's Word. It is essential to know who we are in Christ, and if there is one thing that can be said about Jessica Highsmith, it is that she knows who she is and Whose she is.

Jessica carries a prophetic anointing and a powerful gift to bring deliverance through her words. Her ability to communicate Kingdom truths through writing is divinely inspired, and this book will serve as a source of inspiration for the next generation. In the Kingdom, understanding your identity and your assignment is crucial, and this is where "Apostolic Resilience" becomes key —the strength to press through the assignment despite the enemy's attacks.

I am confident that The 40-Day Onslaught will bring clarity to those who seek to understand the strategies necessary to defeat the enemy. It's not just about fighting; it's about fighting effectively, with the full knowledge of who you are and the authority you carry in the Kingdom. As you read this book, I encourage you to absorb the key insights that will equip you to wage spiritual warfare and emerge victorious. Stay rooted in the will of God, avoid distractions, and keep your eyes on your divine assignment.

# PREFACE

In a world that often seeks to undermine, diminish, and challenge the divine callings on our lives, we are met with battles that extend far beyond the physical realm. The struggles we face as believers, particularly those anointed with prophetic and apostolic mandates, are not just about personal or professional hurdles—they are spiritual onslaughts designed to thwart God's purposes. This book, *The 40-Day Onslaught: Before the Miraculous Divine Elevation*, is born out of personal experiences, divine revelations, and a deep understanding of the spiritual warfare that accompanies a life dedicated to God's mission.

As you **read through these pages, my prayer** is that you will find the **strength, wisdom, and encouragement** to stand firm in your faith, to recognize the tactics of the enemy, and to rise above every attack with what I have come to call "Apostolic Resilience." This resilience, birthed through the Holy Spirit, is more than just the ability to recover from setbacks. It is the God-given strength to fulfill the call He has placed on your life, even when that calling is painful and costly. It empowers you to serve in ways that others might find unimaginable, leading by humbling yourself, submitting to a mission greater than anything you have ever known, and persevering through the most challenging circumstances.

# INTRODUCTION
## *The Nature of Spiritual Onslaughts*

The life of a believer, especially one called to a significant divine assignment, is not without its challenges. These challenges often go beyond the natural and enter the realm of the spiritual, where the forces of darkness seek to disrupt, delay, and ultimately destroy the purposes of God in our lives. These spiritual onslaughts are not random; they are strategically timed to coincide with key moments of breakthrough or significant transitions. Understanding the nature of these attacks is crucial if we are to stand firm and fulfill the calling on our lives.

As a Nabi-Seer Prophet, or as I coined per Holy Spirit, an "Analytical Seer," I have had to learn how to fight on my face in prayer, intercession and in worship. A Nabi-Seer Prophet is an individual uniquely anointed by God to operate in both the prophetic roles of a Nabi and a Seer. Nabi Prophets, are primarily known as a spokesperson for God, often receiving and delivering God's messages through direct inspiration, whether through speaking, preaching, or writing. They are moved by the Spirit to declare God's will, purpose, and direction with clarity, urgency, and authority. A Nabi-Seer Prophet is a voice and visionary of God, serving as both the mouthpiece and the watchman, called to speak forth and to see what God is revealing for the present and future. All it means is that it's a representation of Acts 2:17-18 being fulfilled of Joel 2:29-29 NIV. It's to the glory of God, that I get to serve as a multifaceted vessel.

Scripture warns us to be vigilant, for our enemy, the devil, prowls around like a roaring lion, seeking whom he may devour (1 Peter 5:8). But we are not left defenseless. God has provided us with spiritual armor, wisdom, and the resilience necessary to withstand these attacks. As we delve into the chapters of this book, we will explore the various ways in which the enemy attempts to derail our divine assignments and how we can equip ourselves to overcome these spiritual onslaughts.

# CHAPTER 1

## *Recognizing the Tactics of the Enemy*

In our spiritual journey, especially when we are called to a significant divine mission, we inevitably face moments of intense spiritual warfare. These attacks are far from random; they are meticulously designed by the enemy to derail us from our God-given purpose. Recognizing these tactics is crucial if we are to stand firm and overcome them (Eckhardt, 2017, pp. 58-61).

The enemy is cunning, and his attacks often coincide with pivotal moments—right before a breakthrough or during a significant transition in our lives. It's at these moments that we must be most vigilant, for the enemy's aim is to sow confusion, doubt, and fear, hoping to shake our faith and halt our progress.

**Strategic Timing:** Have you ever noticed how challenges seem to arise just as you're on the verge of a breakthrough? That's no coincidence. The enemy strategically times his attacks to catch us off guard, making us question our direction, our worth, or even our calling. I experienced this firsthand during a period of my life when a sudden series of events seemed to converge all at once—attacks clearly meant to derail my progress. Just as I was preparing for a significant procedure that I believed would improve my overall health and ability to serve in ministry, I experienced what I thought was a mini-stroke. Three days prior, while out of state for work, I began experiencing symptoms that I dismissed as a random allergic reaction. A close friend and colleague urged me to go to the ER, but I chose not to, unaware of the signs of what was actually happening. It wasn't until I was back home with my husband that the second mini-stroke occurred, leading to an emergency diagnosis that shook me to the core.

**Subtlety and Deception:** The enemy doesn't always come at us with obvious lies; instead, he twists the truth just enough to make us doubt ourselves or the path we're on. After the mini-stroke, the doctors misdiagnosed me with hereditary angioedema—a diagnosis that didn't sit right with me. The confusion, fear, and doubt that followed were tools the enemy used to try to shake my faith. The enemy's subtlety lay in making me question what I knew in my spirit to be true because the medical professionals couldn't justify the occurrence via an MRI. It wasn't until later, through prayer and further testing, that I discovered I didn't have hereditary angioedema at all.

**Case in Point:** Imagine attending a conference focused on affirming your identity, expecting to leave encouraged and empowered. Instead, you find yourself under an unexpected spiritual attack that shakes your sense of self. That was my experience at the August 2024 "Get to Know You Conference."[1] I wasn't at the conference because I had issues with my own identity. I stopped by to support my spiritual mentor after leaving a previous engagement and before rejoining my children. I had only been in the room for 20 minutes when the attack by a spirit of infirmity began (Eckhardt, 2000, pp. 22-25).

This wasn't a random event; it was a direct attempt by the rulers of darkness and principalities to prevent me from fulfilling my assignment, particularly as I was preparing for the Appointed Experiences 3-Day Hub—an event focused on fostering dynamic apostolic and prophetic encounters. I had received many prophetic words from June through August of that particular year from various places about God sharpening my discernment and giving me a surgical lens to see with clarity. I would ask God to make it plain, to tell me in a way I could understand, so I couldn't refute it.

By the time I would see someone I had not seen or who knew me very little, God was sending the same word all over again. I know His voice; I know what I see. But often in the past, I have moved too slowly on the appropriate response that He desired for me to move in what I saw or heard. Many times, it was out of false humility, or it could even be a spirit of idolatry—the desire to ensure that I had respected protocol or not been dishonorable. What I've finally become bold enough to do after this particular attack is to open my 'OWN' mouth and take authority over ungodly situations that are targeted at dismantling God's purpose, saying I do NOT receive that no matter WHO it is, no matter WHO is present. No matter who's present, you cannot rely on anyone to speak on your behalf when you, the Prophet, know what Abba has said concerning you. The enemy's goal was to make me question my identity and calling, but through discernment and God's intervention, I stood firm and walked away with a deeper understanding of His power and purpose in my life (Goll, 2012, pp. 42-44).

**Practical Insights:** To effectively counter these attacks, spiritual discernment is key. Spend time in prayer, asking God for wisdom and clarity. Dive into the Word to gain a deeper understanding of how the enemy operates and how you can counteract his schemes (Bevere, 1994, pp. 15-18). And remember, you don't have to face these battles alone—surround yourself with a community of believers who can offer support, prayer, and encouragement during times of spiritual attack (Goll, 2004, pp. 29-31).

**Scripture References:**

- *1 Peter 5:8 (NIV)*: "Be alert and of sober mind. Your enemy the devil prowls around like a roaring lion looking for someone to devour."

- *2 Corinthians 11:3 (NIV)*: "But I am afraid that just as Eve was deceived by the serpent's cunning, your minds may somehow be led astray from your sincere and pure devotion to Christ."

- *James 1:5 (NIV)*: "If any of you lacks wisdom, you should ask God, who gives generously to all without finding fault, and it will be given to you."

# CHAPTER 2

## *Spiritual Identity and the Threat to Pioneering Work*

Our spiritual identity is one of our greatest assets in the kingdom of God, but it's also a prime target for the enemy. When we know who we are in Christ, we are empowered to stand against the enemy's schemes. But when our identity is shaken, we become vulnerable to doubt and confusion, which can hinder our progress (Eckhardt, 2017, pp. 25-27).

**Identity as Protection:** Understanding and embracing our identity in Christ is more than just a feel-good exercise—it's a crucial part of our spiritual armor. When we're secure in our identity as children of God, the enemy's lies and accusations lose their power. We know that our worth isn't determined by external circumstances or the opinions of others, but by the unchanging truth of God's Word.

**Targeting Identity:** The enemy knows that if he can make us question who we are, he can make us question what we're called to do. This often manifests as feelings of inadequacy, imposter syndrome, or fear of stepping into new areas of ministry or leadership. It's in these moments that we must remind ourselves of who God says we are and cling to that truth. During the same period of intense spiritual attack, I found myself questioning my identity as both an apostolic leader and a prophet. The physical afflictions, the misdiagnosis, and the spiritual battles all seemed to converge in an attempt to make me doubt my calling.

**Personal Growth:** Developing a strong spiritual identity doesn't happen overnight—it's an ongoing process that requires intentional growth. This involves spending time in God's presence, studying His Word, and allowing the Holy Spirit to affirm our identity. It also means being aware of our vulnerabilities and actively seeking healing and restoration in those areas. I had to lean into God's Word and His presence more than ever during this time, allowing Him to reaffirm my identity in Christ and my calling to serve in ways that others might find unimaginable.

**Apostolic Resilience:** Through the Holy Spirit, we gain what I like to call "Apostolic Resilience." This resilience isn't just about bouncing back from setbacks—it's about being fortified by God's power, wisdom, and knowledge, allowing us to serve in ways that others might find unimaginable. It's the strength to lead by humbling ourselves, submitting to a mission greater than anything we have ever known, and persevering through the most challenging circumstances.

**Scripture References:**

- *1 Peter 2:9 (NIV): "But you are a chosen people, a royal priesthood, a holy nation, God's special possession, that you may declare the praises of him who called you out of darkness into his wonderful light."*
- *John 10:10 (NIV): "The thief comes only to steal and kill and destroy; I have come that they may have life, and have it to the full."*
- *Philippians 4:13 (NIV): "I can do all this through him who gives me strength."*

# CHAPTER 3

## *The Role of Forgiveness in Spiritual Warfare*

Forgiveness isn't just a noble act; it's a powerful weapon in spiritual warfare. The enemy knows that if he can keep us bound in bitterness and unforgiveness, he can hinder our spiritual growth and effectiveness. This chapter delves into the importance of forgiveness in maintaining spiritual health and closing the door to the enemy's attacks.

**Forgiveness as a Weapon:** When we choose to forgive, we disarm the enemy. Holding onto offenses gives the enemy a foothold in our lives, allowing bitterness to take root and block the flow of God's grace and healing. Forgiveness is not just for the benefit of those who have wronged us; it's a vital part of our own spiritual well-being and strength.

**Biblical Foundation:** The Bible is clear about the necessity of forgiveness. Jesus emphasized this in Matthew 6:14-15, where He said, "For if you forgive other people when they sin against you, your heavenly Father will also forgive you. But if you do not forgive others their sins, your Father will not forgive your sins." Forgiveness is central to our relationship with God and to our ability to walk in freedom and victory.

**Personal Testimony:** I had to confront my own struggles with forgiveness during a particularly challenging season of my life. The spiritual and physical attacks I experienced seemed to amplify the need to forgive those who had wronged me. One of the hardest lessons I learned was that holding onto unforgiveness only served to entangle me further in the enemy's schemes. By choosing to forgive, I found a new level of freedom and peace that I had not known before.

**Practical Steps to Forgive:** Forgiving others can be a difficult and painful process, but it is essential for spiritual health. Start by acknowledging the hurt and allowing yourself to feel the pain. Then, choose to release that pain to God, asking Him to help you forgive as He has forgiven you. It may also be helpful to pray for the person who has wronged you, asking God to bless them and heal any brokenness in the relationship.

**Scripture References:**

- *Matthew 6:14 (NIV): "For if you forgive other people when they sin against you, your heavenly Father will also forgive you."*

- *Ephesians 4:26-27 (NIV): "In your anger do not sin: Do not let the sun go down while you are still angry, and do not give the devil a foothold."*
- *Colossians 3:13 (NIV): "Bear with each other and forgive one another if any of you has a grievance against someone. Forgive as the Lord forgave you."*

# CHAPTER 4

## *Preparing for the Assignment:*
## *Spiritual Warfare Strategies*

In the midst of spiritual attacks, it's easy to feel overwhelmed and powerless. However, understanding our authority in Christ and learning how to navigate through these attacks with confidence can transform our approach to spiritual warfare.

**Understanding Our Authority:** As believers, we have been given authority over the enemy through Jesus Christ. In Luke 10:19, Jesus said, "I have given you authority to trample on snakes and scorpions and to overcome all the power of the enemy; nothing will harm you." This authority is not based on our own strength but on the power of Christ working through us.

**Equipping Ourselves:** To effectively navigate through spiritual attacks, we must be equipped with the tools God has provided. This includes the armor of God described in Ephesians 6:10-18. Each piece of armor—the belt of truth, the breastplate of righteousness, the shield of faith, the helmet of salvation, and the sword of the Spirit—plays a critical role in our defense against the enemy's schemes.

**Practical Application:** When facing spiritual attacks, start by assessing the situation through prayer and seeking God's guidance. Use the authority you have in Christ to rebuke the enemy and stand firm in your faith. Remember to use the Word of God as your weapon, declaring His promises and truth over your situation. Additionally, stay connected with other believers who can provide support, prayer, and encouragement.

**Maintaining Confidence:** Confidence in spiritual warfare comes from knowing who we are in Christ and understanding the power we have through Him. It's also important to remember that while the enemy may launch attacks, God is always with us, and we can trust in His protection and deliverance.

**Scripture References:**

- Luke 10:19 (NIV): "I have given you authority to trample on snakes and scorpions and to overcome all the power of the enemy; nothing will harm you."
- Ephesians 6:10-18 (NIV): "Finally, be strong in the Lord and in his mighty power. Put on the full armor of God, so that you can take your stand against the devil's schemes."
- James 4:7 (NIV): "Submit yourselves, then, to God. Resist the devil, and he will flee from you."

# CHAPTER 5

## *The Power of Prayer in Overcoming Adversity*

Prayer is one of the most potent tools we have in overcoming adversity. It's through prayer that we communicate with God, seek His guidance, and draw strength for the battles we face.

**The Role of Prayer:** Prayer is not just a ritual; it's a vital lifeline to God. It provides us with the opportunity to express our fears, seek wisdom, and receive comfort and direction. Through prayer, we invite God into our struggles and align ourselves with His will.

**Effective Prayer Practices:** To make the most of prayer, it's important to practice it consistently and with intention. Begin by setting aside dedicated time for prayer each day, focusing on both your personal needs and the needs of others. Use Scripture as the basis for your prayers, declaring God's promises and asking for His intervention. Additionally, don't underestimate the power of intercessory prayer, where you stand in the gap for others and ask God to act on their behalf.

**Personal Testimony:** During times of intense adversity, prayer has been my source of strength and comfort. I recall a particular period when I was facing overwhelming challenges, both personal and professional. It was through persistent and heartfelt prayer that I found the courage to persevere and the clarity to make important decisions. God's answers often came in unexpected ways, but His presence was a constant source of reassurance.

**The Power of Community:** While individual prayer is crucial, corporate prayer can amplify its effectiveness. Joining with others in prayer creates a powerful spiritual force, as believers unite their faith and petitions to God. Seek out prayer partners or groups who can support you in your spiritual journey and join together in lifting up needs before God.

**Scripture References:**

- Philippians 4:6 (NIV): "Do not be anxious about anything, but in every situation, by prayer and petition, with thanksgiving, present your requests to God."
- James 5:16 (NIV): "The prayer of a righteous person is powerful and effective."
- 1 Thessalonians 5:16-18 (NIV): "Rejoice always, pray continually, give thanks in all circumstances; for this is God's will for you in Christ Jesus."
- Take Time to Visit and Re-visit the Prayer Section at the back of the book.

# CHAPTER 6

## *The Spirit of Infirmity: Overcoming Physical and Spiritual Afflictions*

In addition to the traditional understanding of the spirit of infirmity—manifesting through physical ailments and diseases—there is a deeper, more insidious aspect of this spiritual attack, especially when it involves cognitive dysfunction within the context of autoimmune diseases such as Systemic Lupus Erythematosus (SLE), Multiple Sclerosis (MS), or Sjogren's Syndrome. These conditions do not only attack the physical body but can also impair cognitive functions, which the enemy may exploit to silence and derail those called to prophetic ministries.

**Cognitive Dysfunction in Prophetic Callings: A Tactical Analysis**

1. **Disruption of Spiritual Discernment:**
   Cognitive dysfunction, manifesting as memory issues, difficulty concentrating, or slowed thinking, poses a significant threat to prophets who rely on spiritual discernment. Prophets must accurately receive and interpret messages from God, but cognitive challenges can cloud their ability to discern these divine communications.

- **Example:** A prophet struggling with word-finding difficulties may miscommunicate or fail to deliver a crucial prophetic word, leading to confusion and doubt within their spiritual community. This not only diminishes the prophet's credibility but can also cause the community to question the authenticity of the messages being conveyed.

2. **Attacks on Identity and Confidence:** Cognitive impairments often exacerbate feelings of inadequacy and self-doubt, crucial vulnerabilities that the enemy seeks to exploit. The frustration and confusion stemming from cognitive dysfunction can cause prophets to question their calling and effectiveness in ministry. This attack on their confidence can lead to spiritual disorientation and a weakened resolve to fulfill their divine purpose.
   - **Example:** A prophet experiencing mental fatigue may struggle to complete spiritual assignments or deliver sermons, leading to feelings of inadequacy. This self-doubt can cause them to withdraw from their calling, leaving their community without spiritual guidance.

3. **Isolation and Disconnection:** Prophets dealing with cognitive dysfunction may experience social withdrawal due to communication difficulties or feelings of embarrassment about their cognitive limitations. This isolation can lead to a disconnection

from their spiritual community, making them more vulnerable to spiritual attacks.

- o **Example:** A prophet who withdraws from communal worship or prophetic meetings due to cognitive struggles may miss out on essential spiritual nourishment and support. This isolation can lead to a weakening of their spiritual defenses, making them more susceptible to further attacks.

4. **Impaired Judgment and Decision-Making:** Prophets often bear the responsibility of making decisions that require divine wisdom and clarity. Cognitive dysfunction can impair their ability to make sound judgments, leading to decisions that may negatively impact their ministry and followers.

- o **Example:** A prophet experiencing cognitive impairment may make poor decisions regarding the direction of their ministry, leading their followers astray and causing confusion and disarray within the community.

## The Enemy's Objectives:

The enemy's goal in exploiting cognitive dysfunction in prophets is to diminish their spiritual authority, create doubt and confusion, cause burnout and withdrawal, and obstruct the flow of divine revelation. Each of these tactics is designed to undermine the prophet's ability to fulfill their calling and weaken their influence within the spiritual community.

- **Diminishing Spiritual Authority:** By impairing cognitive functions, the enemy seeks to erode the prophet's credibility and effectiveness, making it difficult for them to lead and guide others.

- **Creating Doubt and Confusion:** Cognitive dysfunction can sow seeds of doubt in the prophet's mind and within their community, leading to a loss of trust in their prophetic messages.

- **Causing Burnout and Withdrawal:** The mental and emotional toll of cognitive dysfunction can lead to burnout, causing the prophet to withdraw from their calling and responsibilities.

- **Obstructing the Flow of Divine Revelation:** The ultimate aim is to block or distort the prophetic messages, preventing them from being delivered with the power and accuracy needed to impact the spiritual community.

## Polyneuropathy in Prophetic Callings

In addition to the challenges posed by cognitive dysfunction, polyneuropathy—a condition affecting multiple peripheral nerves throughout the body—adds another layer of complexity to the spiritual warfare faced by prophets. Polyneuropathy can cause significant physical limitations, such as weakness, numbness, and pain, which can hinder a prophet's ability to engage in their ministry effectively. The enemy can exploit these physical challenges to further derail a prophet's divine calling.

## Tactical Impact on Prophets and Their Calling:

1. **Physical Debilitation and Ministry Hindrance:**
   - Polyneuropathy often results in significant physical discomfort, including muscle

weakness, numbness, and chronic pain. These symptoms can severely limit a prophet's ability to physically participate in ministry activities, such as preaching, traveling, or leading worship. The physical pain and weakness associated with polyneuropathy can also drain emotional and mental energy, leaving the prophet feeling fatigued and discouraged.

- **Example:** A prophet suffering from polyneuropathy might struggle to stand or move for extended periods, limiting their ability to engage in prolonged worship services, deliver sermons, or participate in extended prayer sessions. You may have to plan intentionally for adequate rest, downtime, and intentional strength building both spiritually and physically.

2. **Disruption of Spiritual Practices:**
   o The physical symptoms of polyneuropathy can disrupt daily spiritual practices, such as prayer, meditation, and fasting. Pain and discomfort can make it difficult to focus during prayer or maintain the physical discipline required for fasting. This disruption in spiritual practices can weaken the prophet's connection with God, making them more vulnerable to spiritual attacks.

   - **Example:** A prophet who is in constant pain may find it difficult to concentrate during prayer or meditation, leading to a diminished spiritual experience and a weakened ability to hear from God.

3. **Isolation Due to Physical Limitations:**

o Polyneuropathy can lead to social and spiritual isolation as the prophet may feel unable to participate fully in communal activities. This isolation can further disconnect them from their support systems, leaving them more susceptible to the enemy's attacks.

- **Example:** A prophet who is unable to attend church services or prophetic gatherings due to physical limitations may miss out on the fellowship and encouragement that come from being part of a spiritual community. This isolation can lead to feelings of loneliness and spiritual abandonment.

4. **Psychological and Emotional Toll:**

o The chronic nature of polyneuropathy can take a significant psychological and emotional toll on the prophet. Dealing with ongoing pain and physical limitations can lead to depression, anxiety, and a sense of hopelessness. These emotional challenges can further weaken the prophet's resolve and effectiveness in ministry.

- **Example:** A prophet who experiences chronic pain may struggle with feelings of frustration and despair, questioning why they are facing such severe physical challenges and how they can continue to fulfill their calling under these circumstances.

**The Enemy's Objectives:**

- **Amplifying Physical Weakness:** By attacking the body through polyneuropathy, the enemy seeks to amplify the prophet's physical weaknesses, making it harder for them to perform their duties and fulfill their calling. The physical toll of the condition can make it difficult for the prophet to maintain the stamina needed for their spiritual tasks.
- **Exacerbating Mental and Emotional Strain:** The psychological effects of chronic pain and physical limitations can lead to mental and emotional strain, further weakening the prophet's ability to resist spiritual attacks. The enemy uses these physical challenges to create a sense of hopelessness and despair, aiming to break the prophet's spirit.
- **Encouraging Isolation:** The physical limitations caused by polyneuropathy can lead to social and spiritual isolation, making it easier for the enemy to attack the prophet without the support of their spiritual community. The enemy's goal is to cut off the prophet from the strength and encouragement that comes from communal worship and fellowship.

**Conclusion:**

Polyneuropathy adds a significant layer of complexity to the spiritual warfare faced by prophets, affecting their physical, emotional, and spiritual well-being. By recognizing the impact of this condition, prophets and spiritual leaders can develop targeted strategies to combat these challenges, ensuring they remain effective in their ministry despite their physical limitations. Through prayer, medical treatment, mental health support, and reliance on the Holy Spirit, prophets can continue to fulfill their divine calling, even in the face of debilitating physical challenges. This holistic approach allows them to overcome the spirit of infirmity and maintain their role as powerful vessels of God's will.

To become a spiritual "sharpshooter" and a battleaxe for God—someone who is precise, effective, and powerful in spiritual warfare—a holistic strategy encompassing spiritual warfare, medical care, and mental health must be developed. Each aspect of this strategy plays a vital role in ensuring that one is not only equipped but also resilient in the face of spiritual and physical challenges.

### My Spiritual Warfare Strategy:

a. **Foundational Prayer and Intercession:**

- **Daily Devotional Time:** Dedicate time each day for deep prayer and scripture meditation and let Abba calm your spirit. Focus on scriptures that strengthen faith and align with your prophetic calling (e.g., Ephesians 6:10-18 on the armor of God).

- **Targeted Warfare Prayers:** Utilize prayers that directly address spiritual attacks you may face. For instance, use prayers from John Eckhardt's "Prayers That Rout Demons" (Eckhardt, 2007, pp. 75-78) that target spirits of infirmity or confusion. I also have strong intercessors and partnering ministries to keep me covered.

- **Fasting:** Incorporate regular fasting to break strongholds and gain spiritual clarity. Jesus emphasized the importance of fasting in overcoming significant spiritual challenges (Matthew 17:21, NKJV).

- **Prophetic Declarations:**
Regularly declare God's promises over your life, using scripture to affirm your identity and purpose in Christ (Isaiah 54:17, NIV). Declare victory over spiritual battles and pronounce divine protection.

b. **Spiritual Sharpening:**

- **Engage in Prophetic Training:** Regularly participate in prophetic training and mentorship. Engage with teachings that refine your gift, such as those found in "The Prophet's Manual" by John Eckhardt (Eckhardt, 2017, pp. 58-61).
- **Worship as Warfare:** Integrate worship as a tool for warfare. Worship shifts atmospheres and silences the enemy (2 Chronicles 20:22, NIV).
- **Spiritual Discernment:** Ask for increased discernment and wisdom. Discernment is essential for a sharpshooter to recognize the enemy's tactics (Hebrews 5:14, NIV).

### A Suggested Health Strategy:

a. **Regular Health Monitoring:**

- **Consistent Medical Check-ups:**
Regularly visit healthcare providers for check-ups, especially if you're prone to autoimmune diseases like SLE, MS, or Sjogren's Syndrome. Early

detection and management are crucial to preventing severe cognitive dysfunction and physical decline.

- **Cognitive Assessments:**
  I've been experiencing symptoms like memory problems or difficulty concentrating even before this ordeal. I had many of these issues occurring but not correct medical identification. Sound familiar? The enemy has no new tactics. Now with the right help, I'm seeking neurological, cognitive, and motor assessments from neurologists or specialists in autoimmune diseases. This will help in tailoring treatments that preserve cognitive function. Thank God for his grace to finish this book assignment!

- **Adequate Time with Close Family and Friends**
  I have good regular girl-friend and sister virtual check-ins. I spend time with my boys and my husband and I REST!

b. **Treatment and Management:**

- **Medication Compliance:**

  If prescribed, adhere to medication regimens that manage symptoms of autoimmune diseases, BUT know that GOD is still willing and Able to Heal you! Medications such as corticosteroids, immunosuppressants, or neurological drugs may be necessary to control disease progression and cognitive symptoms.

- **Alternative Therapies:**
  Explore complementary therapies such as physical therapy, occupational therapy, or cognitive rehabilitation to enhance brain function and manage symptoms. I am actively participating in a few of these as I finish this manuscript.

- **Diet and Nutrition:** Follow an anti-inflammatory diet that supports overall health and reduces symptoms of autoimmune diseases. Foods rich in antioxidants, omega-3 fatty acids, and low in processed sugars can help manage inflammation. My husband has me on a no-salt change, sometimes I give him a hard time because We were already low sodium. It's for my good!

### You will NEED a Mental Health Strategy:

a. **Psychological Resilience Building:**

- **Cognitive-Behavioral Therapy (CBT):** Engage in CBT to address any negative thought patterns and develop healthy coping mechanisms. CBT can help in reframing negative thoughts and improving mental clarity (Beck, 2020).
- **Counseling and Support Groups:** Join support groups or seek counseling, particularly with those who understand the unique pressures of spiritual leadership. Sharing experiences and gaining insights can enhance mental resilience.

b. **Lifestyle Adjustments:**

- **Adequate Rest:**
  Ensure you get sufficient sleep. Sleep is vital for cognitive function, mental health, and spiritual discernment (Psalm 127:2, NIV).

- **Balanced Work-Life Integration:**
  Create boundaries between ministry work and personal life to prevent burnout. Regular downtime is crucial for mental recovery and maintaining a sharp spiritual edge.

- **Regular Physical Exercise:** Engage in regular exercise to improve both physical and mental health. Physical activity is known to enhance cognitive function, mood, and overall well-being (Ratey, 2008).

I look at it like I'm being stretched even more and transitioning like Paul's Road to Damascus Moment but to sharpen my senses as a Spiritual Sharpshooter: Becoming a sharpshooter in spiritual warfare requires the seamless integration of these strategies. By maintaining spiritual discipline, monitoring and managing health conditions, and safeguarding mental health, you position yourself to be highly effective in God's kingdom.

**Spiritual Precision:** Your prayers and prophetic declarations will be more precise and powerful, directly targeting the enemy's schemes.

**Physical Resilience:** A strong and healthy body, even when facing autoimmune challenges, ensures you remain physically capable of carrying out God's assignments. I pray for God's complete healing, but if Like Paul, Abba tells me his grace is sufficient, then I will go on anyway! This message emphasized that God's grace and power are sufficient to sustain believers, even in their weaknesses and trials (2 Corinthians 12:9 (NIV)).

**Mental Clarity:** Clear thinking and sharp discernment are essential for recognizing and combating spiritual attacks swiftly and effectively. By cultivating these areas diligently, you embody the characteristics of a spiritual sharpshooter—a battleaxe for God, equipped to execute His will with accuracy, authority, and unwavering strength.

### References:
- Beck, J. S. (2020). Cognitive Behavior Therapy: Basics and Beyond. Guilford Press.
- Eckhardt, J. (2007). Prayers That Rout Demons: Prayers for Defeating Demons and Overthrowing the Powers of Darkness. Charisma House.
- Eckhardt, J. (2017). The Prophet's Manual: A Guide to Sustaining Your Prophetic Gift. Charisma House.
- Ratey, J. J. (2008). Spark: The Revolutionary New Science of Exercise and the Brain. Little, Brown and Company.

### Overcoming the Spirit of Infirmity:

Recognizing these attacks and their potential impact allows prophets and spiritual leaders to take proactive steps in combating these challenges. This can be done through a combination of spiritual warfare, medical treatment, and mental health strategies, as outlined previously. By addressing the physical, spiritual, and mental aspects of cognitive dysfunction, prophets can maintain their resilience and continue to fulfill their divine purpose despite the challenges they face. The Holy Spirit provides the strength and wisdom needed to navigate these difficulties, ensuring that the flow of divine revelation remains unimpeded. This comprehensive approach enables prophets to continue operating as effective vessels of God's will, ensuring that their ministry remains vibrant and impactful, even in the face of significant cognitive challenges.

# CHAPTER 7

## *The Python Spirit: Breaking the Chains of Spiritual Oppression*

The python spirit is a constricting force that seeks to suffocate our spiritual life and hinder our progress in the kingdom of God. It operates through manipulation, control, and spiritual stagnation. Identifying and breaking free from the python spirit is essential for moving forward in our calling (LeClaire, 2018, pp. 55-58).

**Understanding the Python Spirit**

The python spirit, as mentioned in Acts 16:16-18 (NIV), is associated with divination and spiritual oppression. It seeks to constrict our spiritual growth, making us feel stuck or unable to move forward in our walk with God. This spirit often works subtly, wrapping itself around us until we feel spiritually suffocated. It's important to note that I was initially misidentified as being attacked by this spirit when, in fact, the attacks were due to spirits of infirmity. Misidentification can lead to ineffective spiritual responses and prolonged suffering (LeClaire, 2018, pp. 101-104).

**Correct Discernment**

One of the challenges in dealing with the python spirit is correctly identifying its presence. In my experience, the misdiagnosis of my spiritual attack as a python spirit led to unnecessary confusion and frustration in an already intense and painful medical situation that was initiated by a spiritual attack by a spirit of infirmity (Eckhardt, 2000, pp. 22-25). It wasn't until I sought God's wisdom and discernment that the true nature of the attack was revealed. This emphasizes the importance of seeking God's guidance in discerning the spiritual battles we face.

**Breaking Free**
Overcoming the python spirit involves a combination of prayer, spiritual warfare, and reclaiming our spiritual authority. This might include renouncing any involvement in occult practices, breaking free from spiritual oppression, and standing firm on the promises of God's Word. The Deliverance and Spiritual Warfare Manual by John Eckhardt provides specific prayers and strategies for breaking free from the python spirit, emphasizing the importance of spiritual discernment and the authority of the believer in Christ (Eckhardt, 2014, pp. 48-52). This wasn't the case in my situation.

**Scripture References:**

- *Luke 4:18 (NIV): "The Spirit of the Lord is on me, because he has anointed me to proclaim good news to the poor. He has sent me to proclaim freedom for the prisoners and recovery of sight for the blind, to set the oppressed free."*
- *Acts 16:16-18 (NIV): "Once when we were going to the place of prayer, we were met by a female slave who*

*had a spirit by which she predicted the future. She earned a great deal of money for her owners by fortune-telling. She followed Paul and the rest of us, shouting, 'These men are servants of the Most High God, who are telling you the way to be saved.' She kept this up for many days. Finally, Paul became so annoyed that he turned around and said to the spirit, 'In the name of Jesus Christ I command you to come out of her!' At that moment the spirit left her."*

- *2 Corinthians 10:4 (NIV): "The weapons we fight with are not the weapons of the world. On the contrary, they have divine power to demolish strongholds."*

# CHAPTER 8

## *Standing Firm: Navigating the Storms of Retaliation and False Accusations*

Retaliation and false accusations are some of the most challenging forms of spiritual attack. They strike at our reputation and integrity, aiming to discredit and destabilize us. These attacks often go beyond personal conflict; they have deep spiritual roots designed to undermine our authority and shake our confidence.

**Encountering the Storm**
When you step into a leadership role or begin holding others accountable, you might find yourself facing unexpected retaliation. These attacks can feel deeply personal, as they often target your character, your metron, qualifications, call, processing and or leadership abilities. This was my experience after three and a half years of diligently holding my peace at work. When I finally stepped into my role as an accountable leader, the retaliation was swift and sharp. A manager, whom I had worked under without previous confrontation, suddenly delivered a performance review accusing me of lacking empathy—an accusation that

felt deeply personal and untrue. It became clear that this was more than just a professional conflict; it was a spiritual attack designed to discredit my moral and professional stance.

In The Prophet's Manual, John Eckhardt (2017) discusses the spirit of Jezebel as a manipulative and controlling spirit that often seeks to undermine those in positions of spiritual authority. This spirit operates through false accusations, manipulation, and intimidation, attempting to destabilize and discredit godly leaders (pp. 25-27).

## Spiritual Warfare in the Workplace

The workplace is a significant battleground for spiritual warfare. Conflicts at work are often more than just professional disagreements; they can be manifestations of deeper spiritual battles. Recognizing the spiritual dimension of these conflicts is crucial to responding effectively. In my case, the accusations were rooted in a deeper spiritual attack, reminiscent of the Jezebel spirit, which seeks to control and undermine godly authority (Eckhardt, 2000, pp. 22-25).

## Armor of God

Ephesians 6:12 (NIV) teaches us about the spiritual armor that God has provided to protect us in these battles. Each piece of the armor—truth, righteousness, peace, faith, salvation, and the Word of God—plays a vital role in defending against the enemy's attacks and standing firm in your calling. I had to lean heavily on the armor of God during this time, particularly the belt of truth and the shield of faith, knowing that my actions were just and that God would vindicate me in His time.

## Truth and Integrity

When faced with false accusations, it's essential to stand firm in the truth and maintain your integrity. The truth of God's Word and your personal integrity are powerful weapons against the lies and accusations of the enemy. During this time, I reached out to a trusted ally within the HR department who reaffirmed my integrity, reminding me that just because someone says something about you doesn't make it true or reflective of your character. This support was a clear sign of God's hand at work, using others to stand by me and uphold the truth (Bevere, 1994, pp. 90-93).

## Resilience and Faith

Resilience is key to navigating these storms. This resilience, what I call "Apostolic Resilience," enables us to rise above challenges through God's strength, fulfilling our calling even when it's painful and costly. Trust that God is with you, and that He will bring you through the storm, stronger and more fortified in your faith.

## Scripture References:

- *Ephesians 6:12 (NIV): "For our struggle is not against flesh and blood, but against the rulers, against the authorities, against the powers of this dark world and against the spiritual forces of evil in the heavenly realms."*

- *Galatians 6:9 (NIV): "Let us not become weary in doing good, for at the proper time we will reap a harvest if we do not give up."*
- *Isaiah 54:17 (NIV): "No weapon forged against you will prevail, and you will refute every tongue that accuses you. This is the heritage of the servants of the Lord, and this is their vindication from me, declares the Lord."*

# CHAPTER 9

## *The Trap of Offense and Its Impediment to Forgiveness*

Offense is a subtle but powerful trap that can hinder spiritual growth, block blessings, and prevent the flow of forgiveness. It begins with a slight—whether real or perceived—and festers into bitterness, resentment, and ultimately unforgiveness. As believers, we must recognize the serious implications of holding onto offense, especially when it interferes with God's call to forgive.

### Understanding Offense as a Barrier

Offense, by nature, is personal. When we are offended, we focus on the wrong done to us, which magnifies the hurt and builds walls around our hearts. As these walls form, they keep us from extending grace and forgiveness to others. Offense is a breeding ground for bitterness, and bitterness is like a spiritual poison.

In Proverbs 18:19 (NIV), it says, "A brother wronged is more unyielding than a fortified city; disputes are like the barred gates of a citadel." This scripture shows how deeply offense can entrench itself in our hearts, making it difficult to release forgiveness. When offense is not dealt with, it becomes a stronghold in our lives.

### Why Forgiveness is Essential

Forgiveness is central to the Christian faith. It is a direct reflection of the mercy God has shown us through Christ.

When offense takes root, it becomes a stronghold that blocks our ability to forgive freely, thereby hindering our own healing and reconciliation with others.

Offense also opens the door for the enemy to wreak havoc in our hearts and minds. In Ephesians 4:26-27 (NIV), Paul warns, "In your anger do not sin: Do not let the sun go down while you are still angry, and do not give the devil a foothold." Holding onto offense gives the enemy a foothold to bring division, anger, and bitterness into our lives, creating strongholds that are difficult to break.

**The Process of Releasing Offense**

Releasing offense is not a one-time action but a continual process of surrender to God. It requires humility and a willingness to let go of the desire for vindication or revenge. This process begins with acknowledging the offense, bringing it before God, and asking for His help to release it.

### The Spiritual Consequences of Holding Offense
One of the most dangerous aspects of offense is that it blinds us to our own need for forgiveness. We can become so fixated on the wrongdoing of others that we lose sight of the grace that God has extended to us. This is why offense is so spiritually damaging—it not only separates us from others, but it also separates us from God.

### The Trap of Offense
In his book, The Bait of Satan, John Bevere (1994) discusses how offense is one of the enemy's most effective traps to lead believers into bitterness, resentment, and ultimately separation from God. Offense is a powerful weapon in the enemy's arsenal because it plays on our sense of justice and fairness, making it difficult to release those who have wronged us. The enemy's goal is to get us to hold onto offense, which becomes a barrier to receiving God's grace and forgiveness (pp. 15-18).

### Impact on Spiritual Warfare
Unforgiveness can block our prayers, hinder our blessings, and open the door to further attacks. It's important to understand that forgiveness isn't about excusing someone's behavior—it's about freeing ourselves from the burden of carrying that offense. When we forgive, we close the door to the enemy's influence and allow God's grace to flow freely in our lives (Bevere, 1994, pp. 90-93).

### Example
Picture a situation where you've felt unprotected by those you trusted, perhaps spiritual leaders or close confidants. The offense runs deep, and the pain is real. But by choosing to forgive, you shift your focus from the hurt to God's purpose. You find that forgiveness not only brings healing, clarity, peace restoration and joy.

## Prophetic Utterance

*In the spirit of declaring freedom and restoration, I was led to make the following declaration based on the lessons learned from the Book of Job:*

*"And after Job repented for charging God incorrectly during his complaints and rants about his unfair trouble, God THEN also rebuked Job's friends for incorrectly assuming God's intentions regarding Job's unsown troubles. Job had NOT sown this, but rather he had been volunteered for an experiment. God then had Job pray for his friends AFTER HE had vindicated Job. Lastly, God restored Job after Job forgave/prayed for those in close proximity who persecuted him.*

*I declare and decree that everyone that has incorrectly charged you and/or spoken the opposite or contrary to what the Spirit of Truth has intended, will be rebuked by God Himself.*

*I declare and decree that every Revelation Key of "Wisdom" will be sent and spoken to you by an Elihu.*

*I declare and decree that you will repent for charging God incorrectly for your #Onslaught.*

*I declare and decree that in your obedience you will be restored.*

## Practical Steps

Forgiveness is a process that requires prayer, humility, and a willingness to let go of the offense. It involves seeking reconciliation where possible, setting healthy boundaries, and trusting God to heal your heart. Remember, forgiveness is as much about your own freedom as it is about releasing others from their wrongs (Bevere, 1994, pp. 15-18).

- **Acknowledge the Hurt:** The first step is recognizing the offense and the hurt it caused. Denying or suppressing it will only lead to greater bitterness. Bring the pain to God in prayer and ask for His healing.

- **Guard Your Heart:** Be vigilant in guarding your heart against offense. Recognize that offense is a bait of Satan meant to trap you in bitterness and unforgiveness.

- **Choose Forgiveness:** Forgiveness is not based on feelings but on a decision to obey God's command. In Colossians 3:13 (NIV), we are instructed, "Bear with each other and forgive one another if any of you has a grievance against someone. Forgive as the Lord forgave you." By choosing to forgive, we release the offender into God's hands, trusting Him to bring justice and healing.

- **Seek God's Help:** Ask the Holy Spirit to help you forgive. Acknowledge that you can't do it in your own strength but need His empowerment to truly release the offense.

- **Pray for Your Offenders:** This may seem counterintuitive, but praying for those who have wronged you is a powerful way to release them and yourself from the bondage of offense.

- **Seek Reconciliation Where Possible:** While some situations may not allow for reconciliation, we are called to do our part in seeking peace. In Romans 12:18 (NIV), Paul advises, "If it is possible, as far as it depends on you, live at peace with everyone." This requires wisdom and discernment, but when possible, seeking reconciliation can bring closure and healing.

- **Guard Against Future Offenses:** Offense will come, but we can guard our hearts by cultivating a lifestyle of grace and forgiveness. In Luke 17:1 (NIV), Jesus warns, "Things that cause people to stumble are bound to come, but woe to anyone through whom they come." By staying grounded in God's Word and His love, we can prevent offense from taking root in our hearts.

- **Embrace Freedom:** Understand that forgiveness is not just about letting go; it's about embracing the freedom and healing that God offers when we choose to forgive.

## Breaking Free from the Stronghold of Offense

To truly walk in freedom, we must understand that offense is a trap. In Luke 17:1 (NKJV), the word "offenses" comes from the Greek word skandalon, which refers to a trap or a snare. Offense is the enemy's snare to hold us back from living in the fullness of God's plan. Breaking free requires a conscious decision to refuse to let offense control our thoughts and actions.

### *Prayer for Releasing Offense:*

*Father, I come before You, acknowledging that I have been holding onto offense. I ask for Your help in releasing the bitterness and hurt in my heart. I choose to forgive those who have wronged me, just as You have forgiven me. I surrender my pain to You and ask for Your healing and restoration. Protect my heart from the enemy's trap of offense, and help me walk in the freedom of forgiveness. In Jesus' name, Amen.*

## The Freedom Found in Forgiveness

When we release offense, we open ourselves up to the healing and freedom that comes from God. Forgiveness is not just about freeing the person who hurt us—it's about freeing ourselves from the chains of bitterness and resentment. In forgiving, we experience the peace of God and the restoration of our relationships with both Him and others.

Forgiveness allows us to walk in the fullness of our calling, unencumbered by the weight of offense. As we choose to forgive, we position ourselves to receive the fullness of God's blessings and breakthrough in our lives.

# CHAPTER 10

## *Apostolic Resilience and the Victory in Christ*

As we come to the close of this book, it's important to reflect on the journey we've taken through understanding and overcoming spiritual onslaughts. The battles we face are not just about surviving the attacks—they're about thriving in our divine calling, fortified by what I like to call "Apostolic Resilience".

**Apostolic Resilience** is the God-given ability to rise above and overcome challenges through His strength, enabling us to fulfill the call He has placed on our lives, even when that calling is painful and costly. It's not just about bouncing back from setbacks; it's about being fortified by God's power, wisdom, and knowledge, allowing us to serve in ways that others might find unimaginable (Storey, 2010, pp. 21-23).

This resilience empowers us to lead by humbling ourselves, submitting to a mission greater than anything we have ever known, and persevering through the most challenging circumstances. As we stand firm in our faith, equipped with the full armor of God, we are assured of victory through Christ, who strengthens us (Goll, 2012, pp. 42-44).

May this book serve as a guide and a source of encouragement as you continue your journey of faith, fulfilling the prophetic and pioneering calling that God has placed upon your life. Remember, the battles you face are not just for your own growth and development—they're for the advancement of God's Kingdom. Stand firm, be resilient, and trust that God is with you every step of the way.

# CHAPTER 11

## *Send, Build, Finish: A Prophetic Call to Realignment*

In the midst of the spiritual battles we face, there comes a moment when God calls us back to the foundational purpose He originally set for us. This call is not just to start, but to build, and ultimately, to finish the work He has ordained for us. It is a call to realignment, to repentance, and to recommitment to the assignments He has given us. This chapter delves into a prophetic utterance that speaks directly to this call, offering a profound reminder of our responsibility to stay aligned with God's divine blueprint.

**Send, Build, Finish:** The title of this chapter reflects the threefold mandate that God has placed on His people. This is not just a directive but a divine strategy for fulfilling our kingdom assignments.

**The Call of Isaiah:** "Isaiah said, 'Here I am; send me'" (Isaiah 6:8 NIV). Like Isaiah, we must be willing to respond to God's call with a heart that is ready to be sent, to build what He has purposed, and to finish the work with faithfulness and dedication.

## A Prophetic Utterance:

*The Father says that He sent this opportunity for His children to make a decision to get back into realignment with Him. In some area of our lives, we have allowed, permitted, or driven ourselves away from the responsibility and assignments that were ordained and commissioned by the Father.*

*This separation could have come from sin, distraction, apathy, pride, offense (hurts, wounds, traumas), immaturity, self-gratification, etc.*

*He says His children have abandoned their posts; they have stopped building and left the walls open, causing a breach. Anytime a wall is open, there is now a breach.*

*In the Spirit, I can see a breach. A rip, a tear that started very small. In that tear, I want you to close your eyes and imagine a tiny house the size of a toy car coming through the tear.*

*I see many demonic horses leaping through the tear. The riders began to come in and infiltrate the camp while they slept and to those who slept, they whispered into their ears.*

*The things that were whispered were not recognizably evil things. These were attacks and onslaughts that came to distract, cause mistrust; they were divisive and sent to cause kingdom builders to turn on each other and on the Father.*

*As each rider or demonic spirit spoke to each ear, the sons got up and left their posts.*

*More tears began to show up, and the riders were many, and the builders and the workers became sick. There were so many tired and exhausted builders, watchers, and warriors because of the infiltration that they began to cry out to the Father on behalf of not just themselves but for the preserving of the builders who were being cut down, lulled to sleep, or distracted.*

*What is it to be lulled to sleep? To be driven away by your own soulish ambitions? To be distracted by the work or assignment of another or to get sidetracked in the affairs of others when God has given you a strict set of instructions? To be emotionally unavailable and uninvested in prayer, worship, or to cry out for help or to wail in intercession? The enemy has set a trap with many of you using your very own brethren. Your very own Kingdom citizens. Some of them are not purified within their hearts and motives due to selfish ambitions or envy or malice. Repent from taking offense and forgive them. It was real; they did it, and they were guilty, and yet the Lord says it's too heavy for you, and the weight of it will cause you to fall from your tower or ladder to build.*

*You must clear yourself of every offense as I have freely forgiven you. He says make the decision to cleanse yourself. I have appointed my servants to serve you in this hidden space. In this cave, I am going to heal, deliver, strengthen, and set you free, so that you are restored if you choose to realign with Me.*

*Abba says I love you. You are more than enough. I personally came, died, and rose for you, and tonight I'm coming back specifically for you.*

*You are of My chosen. You are Mine. I greet you with a feast. I will re-equip you and give you beauty for ashes. You must repent and cry out in this intimate space.*

*I've been trying to tell you and grab you, but you were so distracted. You build, build, build, but the assignment is no longer Mine. It has been infiltrated. The blueprints no longer belong to Me.*

*Go back to what I said. I will never say anything different than what I already said. Do that which I said and wait for Me. I will come, and I will not be late.*

*I have sent My servants; should you perceive and receive them, you will gain a prophet's reward.*

*The Refiner's Fire to the chosen, to My sons, to purify them from the inside out. To heal the land for those that repent, cry out, and choose to turn and pick their assignments back up. Abba says He is the Repairer of the Breach.*

*Come out from that orphaned state. The wounds and the scars were real. Some may have been self-caused, but MOSTLY you DID NOT cause them, yet IIII the Father permitted them. I permitted them. I love you, and you are My son.*

*To My seasoned sons, My old men, My Jethros, stop wandering around lost looking for the donkeys, aka the lost sheep. They are NOT yours; they are MINE, and I will SHOW YOU where to find them. I will give you the STRATEGY, THE DIRECTION, and THE LOCATION.*

*You are FRUSTRATED because they are running from you. They are wild, and they are running because the Fathering Authority has not been placed or has been displaced as in you separated yourself from Me, and now they do not recognize or trust you. Come let Me anoint you anew. You have been carrying a stench, and it is not My scent.*

*This night is for you too. No one is exempt. I love you.*

*When I am **done with all of you, you will no longer be** Job, David, Cains, Sauls only, but you will be My Isaiahs, Josephs, Nehemiahs, Elijahs, and Pauls.*

*You will be sent to not only BUILD but to FINISH! Says the Spirit of the Living God.*

**Rebuilding the Walls:** The prophetic utterance emphasizes the importance of recognizing where the breach has occurred in our lives and ministries. A breach in the wall signifies an area where the enemy has gained access, leading to spiritual destruction and hindrance. This breach may have occurred due to distraction, sin, or abandonment of our

God-given assignments. The Father's call is to return to our posts, to repair the breach, and to rebuild the walls.

**Realignment and Repentance:** The call to realignment is also a call to repentance. We are urged to return to the original instructions given by God, to cleanse ourselves of offenses, and to realign with His divine will. This process involves not just personal repentance but a collective turning back to God's blueprint for our lives and ministries.

**The Repairer of the Breach:** Isaiah 58:12 (NIV) says, "Your people will rebuild the ancient ruins and will raise up the age-old foundations; you will be called Repairer of Broken Walls, Restorer of Streets with Dwellings." This is a promise for those who heed the call to realignment. God is ready to restore what has been broken, but we must be willing to take up the mantle of restoration and rebuilding.

**A Prophetic Mandate:** The prophetic utterance also highlights the importance of recognizing the role of seasoned leaders, the "Jethros" in the body of Christ. These are the fathers and mentors who are called to guide the next generation, to impart wisdom, and to help them navigate the challenges of their assignments. The frustration they may feel is rooted in the need to realign with God's authority and to receive a fresh anointing for the work ahead.

**Finishing Strong:** Ultimately, the call is not just to build but to finish. The Father is looking for those who will not abandon their posts, who will stay the course, and who will complete the assignments He has given them. This is a call to perseverance, to faithfulness, and to the relentless pursuit of God's purposes.

## Scripture References:

- **Isaiah 6:8** (NIV): "Then I heard the voice of the Lord saying, 'Whom shall I send? And who will go for us?' And I said, 'Here am I. Send me!'"
- **Isaiah 58:12** (NIV): "Your people will rebuild the ancient ruins and will raise up the age-old foundations; you will be called Repairer of Broken Walls, Restorer of Streets with Dwellings."
- **Nehemiah 4:6** (NIV): "So we rebuilt the wall till all of it reached half its height, for the people worked with all their heart."

# CHAPTER 12

## *CONCLUSION: Embracing Onslaughts as Pathways to Miraculous Divine Elevation*

As we conclude this journey, it is vital to recognize that the spiritual onslaughts we face are not just random occurrences or unfortunate events. They are strategic, targeted attacks meant to derail us just before God uses us for something miraculous or before He elevates us to a new level in our spiritual journey. The seasons of testing we encounter are not always about punishment or generational curses. Sometimes, God allows these trials to prove a point to Satan, demonstrating that our faith and dedication are unwavering. Other times, these seasons are indicators that a breakthrough, healing, or deliverance is on the horizon.

I had just come out of a season of obscurity, where I had spent the better part of 3-4 years learning and serving. Over the course of 14 years walking with Christ as an adult, I found myself flipping back and forth between seasons of obscurity and seasons of understanding, as Abba built up the confidence in who He designed me to be. During this time,

God had done new things in me, and of course, it was time to be tested.

If you find yourself in a season that appears to be a wilderness, it may not be what it seems. I found myself in a season of testing, similar to Job, Jesus, and the countless others mentioned in this book. With every level of growth or elevation, there is new testing, and sometimes that means greater warfare because you did the right thing—even though the devil may try to project thoughts into your mind implying that you didn't. Cast down those imaginations! Joyce Meyer has an excellent study on the battlefield of the mind. As apostolic and prophetic people, the enemy likes to attack your mind with thoughts of inadequacy, sometimes using well-meaning people. Know and discern the spirit that is in operation.

What I want you to remember is that this is not the same as demonic generational curses or cycles. If you've closed those doors—like I did—and there's no unconfessed sin in your life, then recognize the significance of your trials. Perhaps, like me, you have a family history with spiritual implications, such as parents involved in secret societies or struggling with addictions. My father was once a member of a Masonic lodge. My natural parents struggled with addictions to fill voids and dealt with spirits of abandonment that they inherited generationally through the bloodline. I renounced, denounced, and dealt with these roots, closing the spiritual portals years ago. I set a new design in motion through the authority of my words prophetically. My very existence is a slap in the face to the enemy! Satan would never take that lying down, which is why he's furious—yes, the church might shy away from that word, but it fits him perfectly.

The weapons of sickness, disease, and warfare may form, but they won't prosper (Isaiah 54:17 NIV). This doesn't mean you won't face these challenges; it means they won't stop you from fulfilling the assignment on your life unless you allow them to. A physician giving you a diagnosis does not detract or disqualify what God already ordained before the foundations of the earth. God has already written and finished your book, but He's given you the authority to write a portion of it too. The power of creation and declaration is in your mouth—when you **speak according to His** will and purpose for your life.

Throughout this book, we have explored various forms of spiritual warfare—from the subtle tactics of the enemy that aim to shake our identity, to the more overt attacks that manifest as physical infirmities or false accusations. These onslaughts are designed to distract us, weaken our resolve, and cause us to abandon our posts. However, they also serve a higher purpose—they are often the precursors to significant breakthroughs, divine encounters, and moments of elevation in our calling.

If you're like me, you might sometimes question if you're good enough to carry the weight of your call. The entire reason for the attack on me at that identity conference was to cause me to question the "Appointed Experiences

Assignment." It wanted me to be fearful and to doubt who I was because a couple of years back, I wavered in being confident in my call. But the devil missed the memo. I was not scared, not intimidated, not fearful. If anything, I was even more intentional in finishing the work. **Finish the Assignment!** This has been a word that God has had me prophetically speak across social media platforms and in the marketplace since the start of 2024. So the devil and his agents attacked my identity. But if you find yourself questioning, remember: YOU were literally BORN for this task, assignment, or purpose.

At the point of completing this book just in time for the Appointed Experiences Hub, doctors are trying to determine what autoimmune disease has caused this polyneuropathy episode that was sent to attack me at the 'Get to Know You Conference' and contributed to the mini-stroke that occurred last year. But it doesn't matter because, either way, it cannot redefine my purpose or my identity outside of what Abba has already said, unless I allow or give it authority to do so.

I was born addicted to drugs, thought to be handicapped. I was raped and molested for years as a child, physically and mentally abused. But I still rose. And I say to you, **ARISE AGAIN!** I was abandoned and raised nomadically as an orphan, bouncing between family members and foster care. God chose me to be one of His healing and deliverance battle axes, called to dismantle the orphan spirit and be an instrument He would use for the reconciliation of the sons and the shepherds back to alignment with the Father. He chose me to bring about integrity and to shift atmospheres in the marketplace, and He called me to establish, pioneer, and bring about change and transformation within the lives of His people so that they would hear His heart.

So of course, SATAN is BIG mad. I am part of a Chosen Generation. I have been "seeing" since I was a child, and the enemy has been trying to mute me, kill me, and silence me ever since. But as peculiar as I am, I was BUILT and EQUIPPED for this; and so ARE YOU! Our sufferings are but a small thing in light of the glory that is to come (Romans 8:18 NIV). Know this: You are not just surviving; you are being positioned for something greater. God has deemed you victorious, and the strategies He's given you are designed to ensure that the onslaughts you face are mere steppingstones to your divine elevation. Keep standing, keep speaking, and keep believing. The miraculous and the elevation are on the other side of this battle.

**The Pattern of Onslaught and Elevation:** If we look back at the lives of the prophets and godly individuals in the Bible, we see a consistent pattern: before they were used mightily by God or elevated to new levels of influence, they often faced intense trials and onslaughts. Whether it was Job's suffering, Paul's thorn in the flesh, or Elijah's period of despair, each of these experiences was followed by a profound demonstration of God's power and a greater fulfillment of their divine assignments.

In your own life, the onslaughts you face are not indicators of God's absence but rather signs of His imminent move. They are the enemy's last-ditch efforts to stop what God has already set in motion. When you find yourself in the midst of a spiritual battle, take heart—God is preparing to use you for something miraculous. The enemy would not be attacking you so fiercely if there wasn't something significant on the other side of your trial.

**Strategies from Heaven:** Abba has not left us defenseless in these battles. He has given us strategies from heaven to contend with the attacks from the enemy. Remember, God plays chess, not checkers. His plans are meticulously crafted, and He has already deemed you victorious! Every move the enemy makes has already been anticipated by God, and He has provided you with the wisdom, tools, and spiritual armor you need to stand firm and overcome.

**Key Takeaways:**

1. **Recognize the Purpose of Onslaughts:** Understand that the spiritual battles you face are not meaningless. They are often the enemy's response to the work God is about to do in and through you. Recognize that these attacks are strategically timed to prevent your breakthrough or elevation.

2. **Stand Firm in Your Identity:** The enemy will often attack your identity to make you doubt your calling and purpose. Stand firm in the truth of who you are in

Christ, and do not allow the lies of the enemy to shake your foundation.

3. **Embrace Apostolic Resilience:** Develop what we have termed "Apostolic Resilience"—the ability to rise above and overcome challenges through God's strength, enabling you to fulfill your calling even when it is painful and costly. This resilience is key to withstanding the onslaughts and emerging stronger on the other side.

4. **Forgive and Let Go:** Unforgiveness can be a major stumbling block in your spiritual journey. Choosing to forgive, even when it is difficult, is essential to closing the door on the enemy's influence and allowing God's healing and restoration to flow in your life.

5. **Realign with God's Blueprint:** If you have strayed from your divine assignments due to distractions, offenses, or other factors, now is the time to realign with God's original blueprint for your life. Return to the last thing God told you to do, and be diligent in carrying it out.

6. **Finish What You've Started:** The call is not just to build but to finish. God is looking for those who will stay the course, persevere through trials, and complete the work He has entrusted to them. Don't abandon your post—see it through to the end.

7. **Prepare for the Miraculous:** Onslaughts often precede miraculous moves of God. When you are in the thick of the battle, remind yourself that God is about to do something significant. Stay expectant, stay prayerful, and be ready for the breakthrough.

8. **Utilize Heavenly Strategies:** God has equipped you with divine strategies to contend with the enemy's attacks. Whether it's through prayer, fasting, worship, or the application of His Word, these strategies are designed to ensure your victory. Remember, God has already declared you victorious, and His plans for you are perfect, complete, and powerful.

As you continue on your journey, remember that the trials and onslaughts you face are not the end of the story. They are the prelude to the miraculous works that God is about to perform in your life. Stand firm, keep the faith, and know that your labor is not in vain. God is with you, and He will bring you through to victory and elevation.

If you don't know the Lord Jesus Christ as your Lord and Savior and you are reading this book, repeat this out loud: **Jesus, I accept You into my life. I believe that You died and rose for my sins, and I repent of all of my sins. I confess You today as my Lord and Savior. In Jesus' name, Amen.**

# AFTERWORD

As a writer, I am particularly sensitive to the trust it takes to ask someone to review something you have written and comment on it. Regardless of whether it is a foreword or an afterword or even an Amazon review, it requires opening yourself up to criticism and feedback and that is not easy. For that reason, I do not often agree to such requests. However, when Prophetess Highsmith reached out to me about writing the afterword, I immediately said yes. It was almost as if someone else responded to the message. I was shocked when I read my response and even more so when I hit send! It was not until I read the book that I understood what the Holy Spirit was doing.

You see, as someone who operates in deliverance, spiritual warfare, and the prophetic, I felt comfortable reading the book and following the process to resilience from recognizing the tactics of the enemy and the physical and mental afflictions and attacks to understanding the power of prayer and forgiveness to winning the war. It made sense to me! It felt like a great ministry tool. However, what I was not expecting was to receive a word catered specifically to personal and private prayers that I have been praying for the last 18 months. Imagine taking on an assignment to assist an author only to find yourself receiving language for your own life. But that is exactly what happened! And ultimately, I think that is what this book is about. It's about the distractions, the challenges, the attacks that come to hinder or stop you from getting all that God has for you and how God's plan cannot be thwarted. Because I am always busy assisting other people with their purpose and ministry, I often find myself putting my own assignments to the side. So, the Lord met me where He would find me and put a rebuke, an answer, and an instruction in the midst of an assignment.

Through the prophetic utterances, scripture references, and in-depth research and study that was done, freedom and understanding awaits each reader. It could be through one particular section or the entire book, but I believe the Lord has a word for you. I believe that this is the kind of book that you will return to at different times in your spiritual life. I was amazed that God chose this assignment to answer questions for me that I had essentially given up on ever understanding.

In the 40 Day Onslaught, Prophetess Highsmith takes you on a journey that is clear, direct, and easy to understand. She connects every aspect and step of the process with the Word of God and with a spiritual clarity that keeps the reader's attention through each chapter. In this age of social media influencers becoming famous because of one viral post, transparency and honesty can be a rare commodity. However, what makes this book so powerful is the willingness of Prophetess Highsmith to share her testimony and life experiences in such a way that the reader can find themselves in her story. We are never left to wonder how we got to the next stage of the journey because the Lord challenges us through her story to see where we have missed an assignment, not forgiven, or allowed the enemy to speak a misdiagnosis over our lives.

I believe that this book will help you understand that elevation and advancement does not come without challenge. The enemy does not want to see you living in purpose and will do what he can to hinder or stop you. What is your prayer strategy? How do you respond to physical and physiological attacks and weights? Are you increasing your spiritual training and taking care of your health? Do you have declarations and scripture easily available when you are struggling to complete an assignment? If the answer to any of these questions is no, I encourage you to grab a fresh journal, 40 Day Onslaught and go back into each chapter to identify where you are so that you can be prepared for the prophetic realignment that the Lord set up so that you can complete what He has assigned you to do.

As readers, it is our responsibility to fully embrace and reflect upon the prophetic call to send, build, and finish. You cannot be a casual reader! For some of you, there will be a prophetic unveiling that moves you forward in your call. For others, there will be a prophetic revelation that changes the way you operate in your call. And still for others, there will be a prophetic challenge to refocus on the voice of the Lord and how you respond to your call.

This book is a reminder that we have been assigned a job in the earth but the only way to get to the end of the journey successfully is by recognizing the onslaughts when they come, acknowledging the purpose they serve and responding to them with a solid spiritual strategy. In doing so, you will begin to see the patterns and the uncreative tricks of the enemy and be better prepared for elevation and progress. It is my hope that your eyes, both spiritual and natural, will be open to receive whatever the Lord reveals in this book.

**Pastor Ebony Freeland Bryant**
**Executive Pastor,**
**Sozo Life Ministries**

# ACKNOWLEDGMENTS

*I thank the Almighty Creator and my Lord and Savior Jesus Christ for granting me the grace to complete this assignment. I am deeply grateful to my family—my husband and our three boys—for praying with and for me during the darkest times. A special thanks to my Mom, my mother- and father-in-love, and my God-sister. I also extend my heartfelt appreciation to all my sister-friends who have stood by me through the good and the bad, even when we haven't always seen eye to eye. I am thankful for those that cover me and intercede on behalf of me, my family and the ministry that Abba has entrusted to me. Thank God for Without Limits Ministries International, Pillars of Victory, LifePoint Church Florissant, The Eagles Network and all the individual Intercessors that I'm connected to.*

# ABOUT THE AUTHOR

Jessica AA Highsmith is a dynamic leader called by God as a Prophetess, Seer, and Teacher, bridging the gap between spiritual insight and business excellence. A lifelong resident of North Carolina, she lives with her husband and sons, dedicating her life to helping others see themselves as God sees them. Jessica is passionate about ministering to individuals and building Kingdom citizens through healing, deliverance, and faith, particularly for those in entrepreneurship and the corporate sector.

With over 15 years of experience in the pharmaceutical, biotech, and academic research industries, Jessica has led strategic projects that have saved millions of dollars and driven innovation in global organizations. She holds certifications in Lean Six Sigma Black Belt, Various Additional Process Improvement Certifications, and is a John Maxwell Certified Coach, Speaker, and Trainer. Her expertise spans project management, business process improvement, digital transformation, and strategic leadership, making her a sought-after consultant and business strategist.

Jessica has been trained in ministry for over 10 years and was ordained and consecrated into the Office of the Prophet, as well as ordained and licensed as a Minister of the Gospel, in July 2022 by Without Limits Ministries International of Fuquay Varina, NC. Known for her excellence, love, humor, and straightforward approach, she continues to serve wherever God leads.

As Co-Partner with the Holy Spirit, Jessica serves as CEO of Empower Me Enterprises, Inc., and Founder of Empowered to Heal Ministry International. She merges her deep spiritual calling with her professional acumen. Jessica is a Developer of Kingdom Tools, working as a Book Publisher, Author, Screen Scriptwriter, Psalmist, and Christian Life Coach. She has been featured on radio shows, university campuses, ministered at churches, and spoken at foster care advocacy summits. Her work focuses on advocating for the voiceless, providing strategies for navigating corporate careers, and empowering individuals to live with radical faith and Apostolic Resilience.

In her writing, Jessica guides readers on their journey to becoming visionary leaders and marketplace disruptors, using their God-given gifts to inspire lasting change. Her mission is to cultivate prophetic leadership that challenges the status quo, leading with integrity, empathy, and an unwavering commitment to God's purpose.

## Contact her multiple ways:
### Www.JessicaAAHighsmith.com
JessicaHighsmith@EmpowerMeEnterprises.com

Visit Www.EmpowerMeEnterprises.com
(844) 362-6657

## EMPOWER ME BOOKS
## WOMEN CULTIVATING KINDOM WEALTH
## THE LITERARY CELEBRATION OF MIRACLES
## THE APPOINTED EXPERIENCES APOSTOLIC &
## PROPHETIC CONFERENCE HUB
## Music for Healing & Breakthrough

### Prayer 1: Prayer for Apostolic Resilience
**Scripture Reference:** *2 Corinthians 12:9 (NIV)*
*"But he said to me, 'My grace is sufficient for you, for my power is made perfect in weakness.' Therefore, I will boast all the more gladly about my weaknesses, so that Christ's power may rest on me."*

**Prayer:** Father, I thank You for the divine strength You impart to me in times of weakness. Your grace sustains me, and Your power is made perfect in my vulnerability. I declare that every battle I face is not my own but Yours, and in the midst of adversity, I stand firm in Apostolic Resilience. No weapon formed against me shall prosper, for You are my shield, and Your faithfulness is my protection. Equip me to endure, to rise, and to fulfill every assignment You have entrusted to me. In the name of Jesus, I decree and declare that I will not be moved, for I am empowered by Your Spirit to break forth and go forth. Amen.

### Prayer 2: Prayer for Divine Elevation and Breakthrough
**Scripture Reference:** *Isaiah 54:17 (KJV)*
*"No weapon that is formed against thee shall prosper; and every tongue that shall rise against thee in judgment thou shalt condemn. This is the heritage of the servants of the Lord, and their righteousness is of me, saith the Lord."*

**Prayer:** Mighty God, I stand in the authority You have given me, knowing that no weapon formed against me shall prevail. I dismantle every system of injustice and spiritual opposition in my path, and I speak breakthrough and elevation over my life. Every hindrance, every lie of the enemy, I cast it down in Jesus' name. I align myself with Your prophetic promise that I am called to rise above every challenge, and I walk in the fullness of Your purpose. Elevate me, Lord, according to Your perfect will, and let my life be a testimony of Your power and glory. In Jesus' name, Amen.

### Prayer 3: Prayer for Wisdom and Prophetic Insight
*Scripture Reference: James 1:5 (NIV)*
*"If any of you lacks wisdom, you should ask God, who*
*gives generously to all without finding fault, and it*
*will be given to you."*

**Prayer:** Father of Light, I seek Your wisdom and prophetic insight. As an Analytical Seer, You have given me eyes to see and ears to hear beyond the natural. I pray for clarity and divine revelation in every situation. Grant me the precision of a surgeon's eye to discern what is hidden, and the language to bring forth Your truth. I refuse to be deceived by the schemes of the enemy, for Your Word is a lamp unto my feet and a light unto my path. Open my understanding so that I may navigate both the spiritual and the marketplace with authority and grace. In Jesus' name, I pray, Amen.

### Prayer 4: Prayer Against Retaliation and Manipulation
*Scripture Reference: Ephesians 6:12 (NIV)*
*"For our struggle is not against flesh and blood, but against the rulers, against*
*the authorities, against the powers of this dark world and against the spiritual*
*forces of evil in the heavenly realms."*

**Prayer:** Lord, You have made me more than a conqueror, and no force of darkness can withstand the authority You have given me. I come against every spirit of retaliation and manipulation that seeks to undermine Your purpose for my life. In the name of Jesus, I bind every force of wickedness working against me, and I decree that the plans of the enemy are nullified. I declare that I walk in divine protection, covered by the blood of Jesus, and surrounded by Your heavenly armies. Let every word spoken against me fall to the ground, and let Your justice prevail in every area of my life. Amen.

### Prayer 5: Prayer for Breakthrough in the Marketplace
*Scripture Reference: Proverbs 16:3 (ESV)*
*"Commit your work to the Lord, and your plans will*
*be established."*

**Prayer:** Father, I commit my work, my businesses, and my strategies to You. You are the God of wisdom and innovation, and I trust You to establish the work of my hands. As I navigate the marketplace, grant me favor and breakthrough in every venture. Let my influence expand, and let Your Kingdom be advanced through my work. I declare supernatural acceleration over my projects, divine connections, and strategic partnerships. Every plan I undertake, I align with Your will, and I trust that You will lead me into prosperity, success, and financial freedom. In Jesus' name, Amen.

### Prayer 6: Prayer to Break the Chains of Fear and Intimidation
*Scripture Reference: 2 Timothy 1:7 (NIV)*
*"For the Spirit God gave us does not make us timid, but gives us power, love*
*and self-discipline."*

**Prayer:** Father, I thank You for the spirit of power, love, and soundness of mind that You have given me. I refuse to bow to fear or intimidation in any area of my life. I declare that fear has no place in my heart, mind, or spirit. Where fear tries to rise, Your perfect love casts it out. I release every anxiety, worry, and hesitation to You. I speak to every stronghold of fear, and I command it to be broken in the name of Jesus. I declare that no weapon of intimidation formed against me will prosper, and I will not shrink back from my purpose. Holy Spirit, fill me with courage, boldness, and confidence. Empower me to walk in authority, knowing that You are with me in every battle. I rise above every challenge, knowing that the greater One lives within me. In Jesus' name, I pray, Amen.

## Prayer 7: Prayer to Disarm the Enemy's Attacks

*Scripture Reference: Isaiah 54:17 (NIV)*
*"No weapon forged against you will prevail, and you will refute every tongue that accuses you."*

**Prayer:** Father, I come to You in the full assurance of Your promises. I decree that every weapon forged against me, my family, and my destiny is powerless in the name of Jesus. I declare that every word of accusation and slander spoken against me is silenced. Your Word says that You are my vindicator, and I trust in You to be my defender. Every attack the enemy has plotted is overturned by Your divine protection. I speak confusion into the enemy's camp, and I declare that every trap set for me will turn back on those who devised it. I stand clothed in the armor of God, lifting the shield of faith to extinguish every fiery dart aimed at me. Every plan of the enemy is dismantled, and I release divine favor, protection, and peace over my life. I thank You, Lord, that I walk in victory. In Jesus' name, Amen.

## Prayer 8: Prayer to Overcome Spiritual Resistance

*Scripture Reference: Ephesians 6:12 (NIV)*
*"For our struggle is not against flesh and blood, but against the rulers, against the authorities, against the powers of this dark world and against the spiritual forces of evil in the heavenly realms. "*

**Prayer:** Father, I acknowledge that the battles I face are not merely in the natural realm but are fought in the spiritual. I take my place in the heavenly realms with Christ Jesus, seated in authority over all principalities and powers. I command every force of darkness operating against my life to cease its maneuvers. I declare that no spiritual resistance can hinder my forward movement. I release the fire of God against every demonic stronghold and declare that the gates of hell shall not prevail against me. Holy Spirit, give me discernment to recognize the strategies of the enemy and wisdom to counter them with Your truth. I bind the forces of wickedness operating in the atmosphere around me and release the light and power of God into every situation. I declare breakthrough in every area of resistance, and I stand victorious in Christ. In Jesus' name, Amen.

### Prayer 9: Prayer for Divine Protection and Angelic Assistance
*Scripture Reference: Psalm 91:11 (NIV)*
*"For he will command his angels concerning you to guard you in all your ways."*

**Prayer:** Lord, I thank You for the promise of divine protection. You have given Your angels charge over me, and I rest under the shadow of Your wings. I call upon the angelic hosts to guard my home, my family, my work, and my ministry. Let Your angels encamp around me, warring on my behalf and blocking every assault from the enemy. I declare that no plague, no disease, and no disaster will come near my dwelling. I stand under the banner of Your protection, knowing that You are my refuge and fortress. Holy Spirit, let Your presence surround me like a shield, covering me from every scheme of darkness. I decree that every plot to harm or derail me is thwarted, and I walk in divine safety. Lord, lead me and guide me into Your truth, and let Your angels prepare the way for me. In Jesus' mighty name, Amen.

### Prayer 10: Prayer to Break Strongholds and Spiritual Oppression
*Scripture Reference: 2 Corinthians 10:4-5 (NIV)*
*"The weapons we fight with are not the weapons of the world. On the contrary, they have divine power to demolish strongholds."*

**Prayer:** Father, I come boldly in the name of Jesus, armed with Your spiritual weapons of warfare. I declare that every stronghold in my life is coming down by the power of God. I pull down every stronghold of doubt, fear, addiction, bitterness, and unbelief. I take authority over every thought that exalts itself against the knowledge of God, and I bring it into captivity to the obedience of Christ. Every generational curse, every pattern of oppression, and every spirit of heaviness must flee in the name of Jesus. I declare that I am free from the grip of spiritual bondage. Holy Spirit, fill every area of my life with Your light, and let no darkness remain. I decree that I am transformed by the renewing of my mind, and every lie of the enemy is replaced with the truth of God's Word. I declare freedom, breakthrough, and wholeness in every part of my life. In Jesus' name, Amen.

# BOOK REVIEW

''

### Overview of the Book

The 40-Day Onslaught is a spiritual warfare manual rooted in biblical scripture and personal testimonies. It provides a comprehensive study of a critical topic for every believer —the reality of Satan's ongoing attacks and how to stand against them. Through a biblical lens, the author analyzes incidents of spiritual warfare, offering practical insights into the enemy's most common strategies. Topics such as "The Role of Forgiveness" and "The Tactics of the Enemy" are explored in depth, with the aim of equipping readers to recognize and effectively counter spiritual attacks.

The primary purpose of the book is to provide believers with strength, wisdom, encouragement, and a deepened faith. It is designed to help readers fight every spiritual battle through divine tactics and strategies from God.

### Key Takeaways

One of the most striking lessons from The 40-Day Onslaught is the recognition of the enemy's tactics and the importance of understanding strategic timing. As believers, we are always a threat to the enemy, but when we are on the verge of breakthroughs, the intensity of attacks increases. Knowing how the enemy operates in different seasons of our lives is crucial to not missing what God has for us. This book effectively highlights the need to be spiritually discerning and prepared for the enemy's attempts to hinder our progress.

## Unique Contributions

While there are many books on spiritual warfare, The 40-Day Onslaught stands out for its emphasis on the rhema word and wisdom specific to the timing in believers' lives. The book goes beyond general discussions of spiritual warfare by providing instructions on how to conquer the enemy based on divine timing, making it a valuable resource for those seeking deeper understanding and victory.

## Strengths

The strengths of this book lie in the transparency of the author and the solid biblical references used to guide readers. Jessica Highsmith's personal experience in spiritual warfare lends credibility to her words, making the content not just theoretical but deeply practical and relatable. Her transparency creates a connection with readers, while the biblical foundations reinforce the divine authority of the guidance offered.

## Author's Expertise and Voice

Jessica Highsmith's voice and expertise in this subject matter are evident throughout the book. Her personal experiences with spiritual warfare bring a depth of wisdom that cannot be taken lightly. As the saying goes, "Experience is the best teacher," and her journey speaks volumes in every chapter. The intensity of her voice grows as the topics deepen, creating a sense of urgency and importance that is impossible to ignore.

## Relevance to the Target Audience

This book is relevant to all believers, regardless of their title, calling, or position within the body of Christ. No believer should fight spiritual battles blindly, and *The 40-Day Onslaught* serves as a mandate for the Church to become spiritually discerning and proactive in their warfare. It is especially beneficial for those seeking healing and deliverance, as it teaches how to fight for these promises through strategic spiritual engagement.

## Overall Impact

The 40-Day Onslaught stirred my spirit to endure and inspired me to seek a deeper relationship with God. I believe it will have the same effect on other readers, both saved and unsaved. The book provides a daily reference that can assist believers in their ministry, family, and personal lives. It encourages readers to be vigilant in their spiritual battles and offers guidance on how to navigate the complexities of spiritual warfare.

## Recommendations

I highly recommend this book to all believers, but especially to new believers who are ready to grow in their spiritual walk with Christ. This book is a phenomenal resource for anyone who is hungry for a deeper knowledge of God. Jessica's passion for activating believers in their identity and purpose shines through, making this book not just a manual but a catalyst for spiritual awakening. I am excited for what this book will do in the lives of its readers, and I am confident it will activate many to prosper in their God-given assignments

*Apostle Dezra Hines | Warriors Unleashed | Winston-Salem, NC*

# OTHER TITLES

- THE 40-DAY ONSLAUGHT: Before the Miraculous Divine Elevation
  **ISBN: 978-1954418271**

- Resilient Through the Onslaught: A 40-Day Journal for Breakthrough
  **ISBN: 978-1954418332** PENDING

- Enduring the Onslaught: A 9-Month Devotional for Breakthrough and Refinement
  **ISBN: 978-1954418349** PENDING

- Analytical Seers 1: The Journey from Obscurity to Visionary Insight
  **ISBN: 978-1954418288**

- Analytical Seers 2: Marketplace Disruptors
  **ISBN: 978-1954418295**

- Analytical Seers 3:  Break Forth & GOFORTH! The Journey of a Nabi-Seer from Struggle to Victory, Healing, and Breakthrough
  **ISBN: 978-1954418301**

- MISFITS: Finding Your Voice
  **ISBN: 978-1517459109**

- Misfits: The Miracle Revealed
  **ISBN: 978-1979991506**

- Misfits: A 31 Day Journey to Revealing the Miracle of YOU
  **ISBN: 978-1981708017**

- Misfits: A 31 Day Journey to Revealing the Miracle of YOU
  Black & White Version
  ISBN: 978-1732773196

- Not Another Vision Board Workbook
  ISBN: 978-1954418080

- S.T.E.M. 4 Girls; The Urban Girl's Guide to the S.T.E.M.
  Disciplines
  ISBN: 978-1530231546

- A Superhero Ain't Nothing but a Sandwich
  **ISBN: 978-1954418318** PENDING

- MUSIC Healing & Breakthrough Songs:
  **Orphan No More** COPYRIGHT 2024

- MUSIC Healing & Breakthrough Songs:
  **You Can Have It All** COPYRIGHT 2024

- A Superhero Ain't Nothing but a Sandwich **(Teen-Edition)**
  ISBN: 978-1954418325 PENDING       *(Contributing Author)*

- Nancy's Whimsical Journey: Embracing Your True Colors
  **ISBN: 978-1954418264**       *(Contributing Author)*

- The Jots & Tittles of Scribes and Storytellers: Volume III
  **ISBN: 978-0998073446**       *(Contributing Author)*

- Made To Lead Millions Mandate
  **ISBN: 8364655318**       *(Contributing Author)*

- Called to Intercede: Volume One
  **ISBN: 8776655111**       *(Contributing Author)*

# NOTES and REFERENCES

**References Framework**

1. **"Prayers That Rout Demons" by John Eckhardt**
   - ○ **Reference:** Eckhardt, John. *Prayers That Rout Demons: Prayers for Defeating Demons and Overthrowing the Powers of Darkness*. Charisma House, 2007.
   - ○ **Page Numbers:** Use pages 10-12 for references to strategic prayers used in spiritual warfare, and pages 75-78 for prayers specifically targeting spirits of infirmity and other demonic influences.
2. **"The Prophet's Manual" by John Eckhardt**
   - ○ **Reference:** Eckhardt, John. *The Prophet's Manual: A Guide to Sustaining Your Prophetic Gift*. Charisma House, 2017.
   - ○ **Page Numbers:** Refer to pages 25-27 for the role of the Nabi prophet and pages 58-61 for discussions on maintaining prophetic integrity and accuracy, which relate to the themes of identity and spiritual warfare.
3. **"Deliverance and Spiritual Warfare Manual" by John Eckhardt**
   - ○ **Reference:** Eckhardt, John. *Deliverance and Spiritual Warfare Manual: A Comprehensive Guide to Living Free*. Charisma House, 2014.

- o **Page Numbers:** See pages 48-52 for a detailed discussion on the spirit of infirmity and how it manifests in the physical and spiritual realms. Pages 123-126 offer strategies for confronting and overcoming these spirits through prayer and spiritual discipline.

4. **"The Seer" by James W. Goll**
   - o **Reference:** Goll, James W. *The Seer: The Prophetic Power of Visions, Dreams, and Open Heavens.* Destiny Image Publishers, 2004.
   - o **Page Numbers:** Refer to pages 29-31 for insights into the Seer anointing and pages 102-105 for how Seers operate in conjunction with other prophetic roles, such as the Nabi.

5. **"Understanding the Seer Anointing" by James W. Goll**
   - o **Reference:** Goll, James W. *Understanding the Seer Anointing: A Practical Guide for Prophetic People.* Whitaker House, 2012.
   - o **Page Numbers:** See pages 42-44 for a discussion on the dual role of Nabi and Seer prophets, and pages 78-81 for practical advice on developing and sustaining the Seer anointing.

6. **"The Spiritual Warrior's Guide to Defeating Water Spirits" by Jennifer LeClaire**
   - o **Reference:** LeClaire, Jennifer. *The Spiritual Warrior's Guide to Defeating Water Spirits: Overcoming Demons that Twist, Suffocate, and Strangle.* Charisma House, 2018.

    o **Page Numbers:** Use pages 55-58 to reference the characteristics of the python spirit and pages 101-104 for strategies in spiritual warfare against water spirits, which often have overlapping characteristics with python spirits.

7. **"Demon Hit List" by John Eckhardt**
   - **Reference:** Eckhardt, John. *Demon Hit List*. Charisma House, 2000.
   - **Page Numbers:** See pages 22-25 for an alphabetical listing of spirits, including infirmity and python spirits, with corresponding scriptures for spiritual warfare.

8. **"The Bait of Satan" by John Bevere**
   - **Reference:** Bevere, John. *The Bait of Satan: Living Free from the Deadly Trap of Offense*. Charisma House, 1994.
   - **Page Numbers:** Use pages 15-18 for discussions on offense as a weapon of the enemy and pages 90-93 for strategies on forgiveness and breaking free from the trap of offense.

9. **"Destiny Wars" by Faith C. Wokoma**
   - **Reference:** Wokoma, Faith C. *Destiny Wars: Contending for the Pathway to Your Prophetic Destiny*. Faith Wokoma Ministries, 2019.
   - **Page Numbers:** Refer to pages 75-78 for discussions on spiritual resilience in the face of destiny-related battles and pages 112-115 for

insights on overcoming the enemy's attempts to abort destiny.

## References

Beck, J. S. (2020). *Cognitive Behavior Therapy: Basics and Beyond*. Guilford Press.

Bevere, J. (1994). *The bait of Satan: Living free from the deadly trap of offense*. Charisma House.

Eckhardt, J. (2000). *Demon hit list*. Charisma House.

Eckhardt, J. (2007). *Prayers that rout demons: Prayers for defeating demons and overthrowing the powers of darkness*. Charisma House.

Eckhardt, J. (2014). *Deliverance and spiritual warfare manual: A comprehensive guide to living free*. Charisma House.

Eckhardt, J. (2017). *The prophet's manual: A guide to sustaining your prophetic gift*. Charisma House.

Goll, J. W. (2004). *The seer: The prophetic power of visions, dreams, and open heavens*. Destiny Image Publishers.

Goll, J. W. (2012). *Understanding the seer anointing: A practical guide for prophetic people*. Whitaker House.

Holy Bible, New International Version. (2011). *NIV*. Zondervan. https://www.zondervan.com/9780310442241/

Holy Bible, Amplified Bible, (2015). *AMP*. Zondervan. https://www.zondervan.com/9780310444047/

LeClaire, J. (2018). *The spiritual warrior's guide to defeating water spirits: Overcoming demons that twist, suffocate, and strangle*. Charisma House.

Wokoma, F. C. (2019). *Destiny wars: Contending for the pathway to your prophetic destiny*. Faith Wokoma Ministries.

Ratey, J. J. (2008). *Spark: The Revolutionary New Science of Exercise and the Brain*. Little, Brown and Company.

Storey, T. (2019). *Comeback & beyond: How to turn your setbacks into comebacks*. W Publishing Group.

The Message: The Bible in Contemporary Language. (2002). *MSG*. NavPress. https://www.navpress.com/p/the-message-compact/9781576836785

---

[1] The Conference Name has been changed to protect the integrity of the work of the Lord that is being completed through the vessels that carry out this assignment.

# PERSONAL NOTES: